FREEDOM AND RESPONSIBILITY

A Biological View of Some Problems of Democracy

A LECTURE AT MILTON ACADEMY
ON THE
ALUMNI WAR MEMORIAL FOUNDATION
MAY 31, 1934

Freedom and Responsibility

A Biological View of Some Problems of Democracy

BY

EDWIN GRANT CONKLIN

Princeton University

BOSTON AND NEW YORK

HOUGHTON MIFFLIN COMPANY

The Riverside Press Cambridge

1935

The Riverside Press
CAMBRIDGE · MASSACHUSETTS
PRINTED IN THE U.S.A.

THE ALUMNI
WAR MEMORIAL FOUNDATION

AT MILTON ACADEMY

STATEMENT OF THE PLAN
Adopted March 7, 1922

THERE has been established at Milton Academy, in memory of the twenty-two alumni of the School who gave their lives in the World War, a permanent Foundation for lectures and informal conferences dealing with the responsibilities and opportunities attaching to leadership in a democracy. It is intended that the lectures shall be given and the conferences shall be led by men of preëminent ability and attainment in various fields of political or commercial administration or professional work, and that the Foundation shall provide an income adequate to the payment of appropriate stipends to such men, and for the publication in suitable form of the lectures delivered whenever such publication shall be authorized by the Head Master and the Executive Committee.

It is further provided that the names of the men commemorated shall be recorded on a tablet to be placed in the Chapel at Milton Academy, and that this tablet shall bear a symbolic device in bas relief, expressive of the spirit of the memorial and adapted for reproduction in miniature on all books and documents in which the further development of the memorial shall from time to time find expression.

Such a memorial as this will never grow old or wear out or be forgotten. Its full strength may be applied over and over again through the years to come to the solution of problems like those which led our country into the war, and to whose solution the men we commemorate intended their sacrifices to contribute.

CONTENTS

FREEDOM AND RESPONSIBILITY

A Biological View of Some Problems of Democracy

FREEDOM AND RESPONSIBILITY

I

Biological Foundations of Society

MY predecessors in this lectureship have been representatives of different professions — statesmen, diplomatists, publicists, generals, educators, bishops. I wish to consider with you the foundations of society and the present crisis in civilization from the standpoint of a scientist, and more specifically of a biologist.

1. *The Zoölogical Position of Man*

Biologically man is an animal, a vertebrate, a mammal, although there are some persons who deny this classification. John Fiske used to tell of a man who became indignant when told that he was a mammal and exclaimed, 'I am not a mammal, nor the son of a mammal'; Fiske added that he had probably been brought up on a bottle. Whatever more we may be, we cannot successfully deny our animal relationships. Man is not only a mammal, he is also a member of the order of primates, of the family Hominidæ, the genus *Homo* and the species *sapiens*. Zoölogists hold that all men at present belong to a single species, genus, and family, but in past geological times there were probably at least six different species and genera in the human family, ranging from creatures of low brow, heavy jowl, and shuffling gait up to the modern species. Extinct genera and species of Hominidæ so far discovered are, in the probable order of their appearance, *Pithecanthropus erectus* of Java, *Sinanthropus pekingensis* of China, *Eoanthropus dawsoni* of England, *Paleoanthropus heidelbergensis* of Germany, *Homo rhodesiensis* of South Africa, *Homo neanderthalensis* of western Europe and perhaps of Asia Minor. No doubt other extinct species remain undiscovered as yet. During hundreds of thousands of years there has been a general trend in the human family toward more erect posture, freeing of the hands from locomotion, enlargement of brain, increasing intelligence, closer social organization and ever larger social units.

2. *Resemblances and Differences of Human Races*

Man is the most widespread of all the higher animals, and it is therefore an extraordinary fact that in all regions of the earth he exists at present as a single species, genus, and family. There are three chief races of mankind, white, yellow, and black, many minor races of intermediate colors and characters, some four hundred well recognized sub-races and tribes, and nearly two thousand million individuals, but the close relationship of all these is shown by the

fact that all human types are able to inter-
breed and give rise to fertile offspring. All
of these various races are much more alike
biologically than different; consequently,
for the sake of economy of thought and
word, when comparing them, we emphasize
their differences rather than their more
numerous resemblances. Indeed, overem-
phasis on the differences among existing
races of mankind has led to many bitter
hostilities and race wars. It would be well
if all men could be made to realize the great
gap which separates the most primitive
races of existing men from the highest
animals, and the close relationship of all
races and classes of mankind.

The differences among Africans, Asians,
and Europeans have sometimes been mag-
nified to such an extent that these races
have been classed as separate species, but
'species' is a biological concept and there is
no doubt among biologists that all human

races belong to a single species. Advocates of African slavery and of white supremacy used sometimes to deny that the Negro is human, but their mulatto offspring scientifically demonstrated the contrary. Even within the white race distinctions between certain sub-races, such as Nordics and Alpines, 'Aryans' and Jews, have been exaggerated beyond all science and reason. Biology proves conclusively that all human races belong to a single species and that the differences between races and sub-races are relatively small as compared with their important resemblances. For example, all races of men have essentially the same biological structures, functions, diseases, emotions, instincts, etc.; they even have the same number of chromosomes in all their cells and many genes or inheritance units are identical in all races. Undoubtedly all men are blood relatives with most of their inherited traits of body and mind fundamentally similar, although showing many minor differences. Even intellectual and social traits are so much alike in all races that their members are often educated in the same schools, successfully follow the same occupations and professions, and in general co-operate harmoniously in the same society.

When we consider the, to us, revolting or irrational customs of other races, such as the worship of sticks or stones by some, or of snakes and bulls by others, or of war lords and emperors by still others, we are ready to exclaim,

> 'East is east and west is west,
> And never the twain shall meet.'

But when we see that members of these same races when reared and educated in other countries adopt the *mores* of those countries, we realize that these differences are the results of environment and social custom rather than of hereditary and racial differences. Science supports the Scriptures in holding that 'God hath made of one blood all nations of men.' In these times of racial, national, and social antagonisms it is important to realize that all men are by nature brothers.

On the other hand, a great intellectual and social gulf separates all modern men from their nearest animal relatives, the anthropoid apes. Although there is abundant evidence that mankind and apes belong to a common evolutionary stem, yet the biological differences between them are so great that zoölogists classify them into different species, genera, and even families, while in mind, society, and culture man belongs in a different class, almost in a different world from all other living things.

What an extraordinarily fortunate thing it is that in all parts of the world mankind exists as a single species, genus, and family! If to the present racial and national conflicts among men there were to be added wars between closely related but competing species and genera, the present disturbed state of the world would in comparison be counted 'peace, perfect peace.' Fortunate it is for mankind that we have no rational or really dangerous animal competitors for possession of the earth, fortunate that 'the earth is the Lord's and he hath given it to men.' When I reflect upon the great differences which separate mankind from all other living things, in spite of former evolutionary connections, I think that I can better understand and appreciate the words of a prayer which I used to hear as a boy, 'We thank thee, Lord, that thou hast made us *men.*'

3. *The Human Struggle for Existence*

We do not know how or why the former species and genera of men became extinct, but since some of them lived through great

changes in the earth and its climate, including one or more glacial periods, since
they had learned to live in caves, make
fire, use weapons, and kill beasts for food
and clothing, it does not seem probable that
they were exterminated by changes in climate nor by beasts of prey. More probably
they disappeared through competition with
more intelligent and better organized societies of men until finally only the present
species remained.

This process of competition, with elimination of the less intelligent and co-operative
types of the present species, has gone on for
many thousands of years and is still active,
although greatly limited of late by certain
social customs. Competition has led to the
seizing of the best parts of the earth by the
most aggressive and progressive types and
the expulsion of others to the less desirable
places, such as Arctic areas, desert wastes,
tropical jungles, and barren mountains; or

within a single society to slums, ghettoes, and marginal lands. It has also led to the enslavement or exploitation of certain races or tribes or classes by others, this being in accordance with

'Nature's simple plan,
That those should take who have the power,
And those should keep who can.'

But with the growth of intelligence and morality among men, this law of the jungle gives place more and more to the law of humanity. The fittest are no longer merely the strongest and fiercest, but rather the wisest and most co-operative. The survival of the fittest is still the great law of life, but there are several kinds of fitness; physically the fittest are the most viable and most capable of leaving offspring, mentally the fittest are the most rational, socially the fittest are the most co-operative and ethical. It was by his superior intelligence and social organization and not by superior strength that primitive man was able to overcome great beasts of prey, and by the same means modern man supplanted more powerful and brutish species of men.

Every society, whether of animals or men, is founded upon the mutual co-operation and benefit of its members. In the most primitive societies the number of individuals that can thus co-operate is relatively small. Among social insects the members of a colony of ants or bees are all the offspring of one mother, and probably the members of the earliest human and prehuman societies were close blood relatives. Between different colonies of ants or tribes of primitive men there are frequent hostilities and little or no co-operation. It is a notable fact that as men rise in intelligence and morality larger and larger social units are possible. No doubt the entire human race could co-operate peacefully in a single world-society if it were genuinely rational and ethical. But at present the relations existing between nations are much like those which once prevailed between colonies and tribes. The struggle of nations for possession of lands, or natural resources, or good markets, or strategic military positions is as keen today as it was in ancient tribal wars; indeed, as populations increase and the earth becomes more crowded, as science advances and the means of warfare are multiplied, this struggle of nations for 'a place in the sun' will become more all-inclusive and dangerous unless controlled by reason, ethics, and the realization that in the long run co-operation is more profitable than conflict.

4. *Birth and Growth of Intelligence and Freedom*

The lowest organisms, both plants and animals, show relatively little freedom of action. Their responses to stimuli are generally constant under usual conditions, and these responses are known as *reflexes* or *tropisms*. And yet even here there is a certain degree of modifiability of behavior, depending upon internal conditions or physiological states. For example, a Paramecium that has bumped into the surface of the water in a capillary tube and then backed away many times will finally bend its body so that it can turn around in the tube and swim in the opposite direction. In short, its responses are not absolutely fixed. A Stentor placed in a solution of India ink will contract so as to shut out the ink, and then will gradually expand and if the ink is still there will again contract. After repeated contractions and expansions, it no longer repeats this useless response, but pulls loose from its point of attachment and swims away. Such modifiable behavior is wholly different from that of any nonliving thing and it marks the beginning of alternative action and ultimately of what we call free or voluntary acts.

With the development of associative memory in higher animals (and all animals that can learn anything have associative memory), the results of 'trial and error' are remembered and such memories become important factors in shaping behavior whenever alternative courses of action are open. This ability to act in response to remembered experience is what we call *freedom* from fixed, mechanistic action, and the remembering of failures and successes in past 'trials and errors' and ability to avoid the one and follow the other is what we call *intelligence*. A cat or dog that has learned to open a door by turning a button or a horse that has learned to open a gate by lifting a latch is just as intelligent with respect to that one act as a man is. But there is little evidence that cats or dogs or horses are able to generalize their experiences and to apply their knowledge of buttons or latches to other kinds of fastenings. This ability to generalize, to see fundamental resemblances in spite of superficial differences, leads to what we call abstract thought and *reason*. Of course both freedom and intelligence vary greatly in different animals and in the same individual at different stages of development. They are relatively slight in human infants and in those who remain infantile throughout life, but they rise to a maximum in normal adults. Men are never absolutely free nor perfectly intelligent, but the more intelligent they are the freer they are. Human freedom is not uncaused activity, but rather the ability to use intelligence and reason as causes of action in the choice between alternatives which are offered. The will is not 'a little deity encapsuled in the brain,' but rather the totality of all those remembered experiences, successes and fail-

ures, rewards and punishments, admonitions
and examples, which influence behavior.

5. *Fundamental Needs and Satisfactions*

The primary needs of all animals, including man, are nutrition, reproduction, defense; all animals find the satisfaction of
these needs through tropisms or instincts
which are modified or directed by the
method of 'trial and error'; that is, by experiment and the elimination of unsatis-
factory responses and conditions and the
selection of satisfactory ones. This implies
ability to distinguish and select or, speaking
objectively, to respond positively to some
stimuli and negatively to others, which the
biologist calls 'differential sensitivity.' And
this is the beginning of intelligence, reason,
judgment, and purpose in man. In every
human being these higher psychic functions
develop out of the differential sensitivity of
germ cells and embryos. When develop-

ment has reached the stage of intelligence, which is capacity to profit consciously from experience, and purpose, which is ability consciously to seek satisfaction, these become potent factors in shaping behavior and in seeking and finding physical, intellectual, and social satisfactions.

In addition to the animal satisfactions of nutrition, reproduction, and defense, intelligent and social human beings seek the intellectual satisfactions of curiosity, imitation, experiment, and adventure; the æsthetic satisfactions of play, beauty, harmony, and progress; and the social satisfactions of union for defense, fellowship in service, leadership or discipleship. These socially integrative satisfactions are often counterbalanced by disintegrative ones, such as selfishness, greed, and combativeness, which tend to break up society into smaller units of race, nation, or class, which conflict with or war on one another.

In higher animals and man these internal or subjective needs and satisfactions are known as *emotions*, and they are the ultimate sources of simple acts and of complex behavior. Anyone who has much acquaintance with dogs or horses knows that many of their emotions are essentially like our own. Hunger and thirst, pain and pleasure, fear and joy, hate and love, jealousy and confidence are similar in kind, if not in degree, to corresponding human emotions. Indeed, man resembles other animals much more in his instincts and emotions than in intellect or reason, and as instincts and emotions are vastly older than intelligence, so also they are more potent in shaping and directing behavior. Intelligence and reason are vastly superior to 'trial and error' as means of finding satisfaction, and yet in human behavior there is frequent conflict between emotion and reason. Indeed, in crises men often cease to be intelligent or rational beings and are guided wholly by emotion. The greatest dangers that threaten society today are emotionalism, sensationalism, irrationalism. The basal needs, instincts, and emotions of men will ever demand satisfaction, but unless they are directed by intelligence and reason there is little hope for human progress.

6. *Principles of Progress*

That there has been progress through the ages no one who takes the long backward look can doubt. No more can one doubt that there has been progress in the development of an individual from a germ cell. All forms of development, whether of an individual, a race, or society, consist in progressive specialization and co-operation; these are everywhere and always the companion principles of progress. The development of an egg cell to an adult body or of the differential sensitivity of a germ cell into conscious intelligence and purpose, or of a primitive race of men into the modern races, or of the society of savages into that of civilized men — all these different developments follow the same fundamental principle of increasing complexity of organization through increasing specialization of constituent units. But everywhere as specialization increases there is corresponding danger of decrease of co-operation of these units or parts. Thus specialization tends to outrun co-operation, and when the disparity between these reaches a critical point either further specialization must cease, or the organism (body or society) must undergo de-differentiation or division into smaller units, or it will cease to exist. Development may be retrogressive as well as progressive; many species are the degenerate descendants of more highly organized forms, many have become extinct; and the same is true of human species, races, and social groups.

Although in this respect as in so many others there is a close parallelism between the biological individual and the social unit, nevertheless human society is neither as highly differentiated nor as firmly integrated as are the organs of any one of its individual members. The loss of any member of society is less serious than the loss of the heart or brain of an individual, and if any society is immortal it is because its individual members are replaceable by others, whereas the loss of any vital part of a person leads to the death of all other parts. Likewise social integration is so loose that there is continual danger of societies breaking up into smaller groups, such as racial, sectional, political, religious, and occupational classes.

This parallelism between the life and development of an individual and of society can be illustrated by many instances. For example, biological progress, whether

of the individual or the race, always consists
of increasing differentiation and integration;
social progress always consists of increasing
specialization and co-operation; everywhere
degeneration and death, whether of an
individual, a species, or a society, are the
results of a loss of balance between these
companion principles of progress. Professor
Minot once said, 'Death is the price which
we pay for our differentiation'; that is,
germ cells and one-celled organisms with
relatively few differentiations are poten-
tially immortal. Some lower animals are
able to undergo rejuvenation by a process
of de-differentiation, but in man and all
higher animals progressive differentiation
leads inevitably to the death of the individual, because effective co-operation or
integration of constituent parts fails. In
societies of ants, bees, and termites a balance
has been reached between differentiation
and integration among the members of the

colony which has permitted species to exist in a nearly static condition for millions of years. But wherever specializations are rapidly increasing, as in human societies, effective integration is endangered.

7. *Biological and Social Balance*

Life and society with all of their functions and processes persist only by the preservation of balance between opposing forces or contrasting principles. Life itself lasts only as long as there is a proper balance between the organism and the environment, between anabolism, or the process of building up, and katabolism, or breaking down, between life and death, for the parts of every living thing are continually forming and dying. It is strictly true of every one of us, as Saint Paul said of himself, 'I die daily'; or as Mrs. Browning wrote, 'All our life is mixed with death.'

Our psychic lives are also dependent on

the preservation of balance between in-
stinct and intelligence, emotion and reason,
safety and adventure, realism and idealism.
Likewise social life and growth in general
depend upon the preservation of a proper
balance between the individual and society,
between freedom and responsibility, rights
and duties, radical and conservative tendencies. And in every phase of society we find
similar opposing tendencies which must be
brought into balance if that phase is to
endure and progress. Thus in economics
there is the necessary balance between pro-
duction and consumption, between labor
and capital, agriculture and industry, individual initiative and collectivism, etc.

Indeed, life and society in all of their as-
pects are as delicately balanced between
opposing forces as is a tight-rope walker
over Niagara gorge. As vital balance is the
most important factor in the life of an
organism, so mental balance or judgment is

the most valuable feature in the psychic life, and social balance the most necessary factor in social progress. The chief problems of society concern the maintenance of a proper balance between the individual and the group, between freedom and responsibility, liberty and duty, progress and stability. Fanatical extremes of individualism or socialism, democracy or autocracy, fascism or communism, find no successful parallels in biology, where life and progress consist in compromise, balance, adaptation.

II

Great Movements in Human History

To the casual observer human history may seem to be an eternal struggle for existence and supremacy on the part of individuals, nations, and races. One goes up and another down. In the pessimistic language of Ecclesiastes, 'That thing that hath been, it is that which shall be;............

and there is nothing new under the sun.' History thus regarded as a record of unconnected events is comparable to the science of biology before the theory of evolution, when every species was regarded as a distinct and separate creation. But the evolutionary view of history, like that of organisms, gives meaning to much that is otherwise meaningless. In the history of man, as well as of animals and plants, many events lead nowhere except to mere diversity and into blind alleys and failure; others lead to increasing fitness and progress.

1. *The Growth of Individual and Social Freedom*

Neglecting casual, confused, and temporary movements, what have been some of the main currents in human history? Within the period of recorded history one of the most evident movements has been the birth and growth of physical, intellectual, political, and spiritual freedom, and the gradual liberation of man from the dominance of nature and the tyrannies of men. From the earliest times human beings have been learning how to circumvent the severities of climate, to make plants and animals subservient to their needs, to control many natural forces and processes and thus to acquire greater freedom from the supremacy of nature. More slowly and intermittently they have been acquiring freedom from human bondage. Some of the oldest human records depict societies consisting of absolute monarchs, or small ruling groups, and multitudes of abject slaves. All the great civilizations of the past were founded on slavery and their great monuments were in the main the work of slaves. Gradually through long centuries there developed amelioration of the severities of slavery and an increasing degree of freedom for the slave. Largely as a result of long struggles and bloody revolutions there are today no countries that could be called civilized in which a formal system of slavery exists, but in all societies there are necessarily leaders and followers, those who plan and those who carry out, those who command and those who obey. In short, there can be no social organization without such differentiation and integration. The chief difference between a free and a slave society is that in the former the distinction between leaders and followers is based upon the natural abilities and capacities of men, whereas in the latter it is based on arbitrary force, rigid class distinctions, or accidental advantage. Even in so-called free societies relics of slavery still persist; autocratic employers sometimes assume the powers of absolute dictators and treat their subordinates as slaves. Nevertheless, there has been a remarkable growth of freedom from slavery in the history of mankind.

This applies, not merely to freedom from involuntary servitude, but also to the later acquisition of intellectual and spiritual freedom. Freedom of thought and speech and press have been so recently acquired that they have not yet become as firmly fixed in society as freedom from physical slavery, and in social crises such freedom is often restricted or abolished for a time. But if history teaches anything it is that such restrictions are mere eddies in the main current of human progress.

Associated with this birth and growth of social freedom has gone the ever-increasing demand for equality of rights, justice, and opportunity for all men and the growing recognition of the fact, so evident to the biologist, of the universal brotherhood of men. These three great movements in human history toward physical, intellectual, and social freedom may be summarized in the one word 'democracy.'

2. *Is Democratic Freedom Feasible or Desirable?*

Our own government is the greatest and one of the oldest of existing democracies and to Americans generally democracy is a kind of religion. The Declaration of Independence, which is the charter of our democracy, 'holds these truths to be self-evident, that all men are created equal'; that is, 'that they are endowed by their Creator with certain inalienable rights; that among these rights are life, liberty and the pursuit of happiness. That to accomplish these purposes governments are instituted among men, deriving all their just powers from the consent of the governed.' Here are the foundation principles of democracy, which are summarized more concisely in the motto of France — 'Liberty, Equality, Fraternity.'

At the close of the greatest war in human history, which we hoped was waged 'to make the world safe for democracy,' we find free governments in many places giving way to autocracies and dictatorships. Representative government is denounced and abandoned in Russia, Italy, Germany, Austria, and it is certainly greatly limited and weakened in many other countries. We may well ask, Is democracy feasible or desirable in the present state of the world? There are many who assure us by word or deed that it is not.

In his book, 'The Decline of the West,' Spengler, the German historian and philosopher, maintains that civilizations, like organisms, have life cycles, starting with birth and ending with decay and death. He compares Classical, Indian, Arabian, and Western cultures and finds that all pass from barbarism, through feudalism, absolutism, and revolution, to democracy, and then to Cæsarism and decay. In his last book, 'The Hour of Decision,' he claims that the growth of democracy has led logically to liberalism,

socialism, communism, and bolshevism, and
that only a return to 'Prussianism' — that
is, fascism or Hitlerism — can save civilization. In view of the excesses of these autocratic systems, their denial of intellectual
and spiritual freedom, their cultivation of
racial and international hate, and their
glorification of force and war, we may well
inquire whether civilization is worth saving
at such a price.

Have we then misread the lesson of
history and mistaken for a main current
what may be only an eddy or backwash in
the stream? Is democracy practicable or desirable in the modern world? Certainly a
democracy like that of the city-states of
ancient Greece, or of the old New England
town meeting, is not possible except in a
small community; in all large populations it
must be replaced or supplemented by representative government, but as long as representatives are the free choice of the

people, the form of government is truly democratic.

The failures of democratic government are only too evident. Ignorance, selfishness, greed, lack of public spirit are widespread among people and public officials. In times of stress there is general impatience with the slow processes of representative government, which is often responsive to lobbies or mobs rather than to the will of the majority. In national crises we welcome a strong leader or even a dictator and hope for an early adjournment of Congress. The fact is that all forms of government must have strong leaders, especially in emergencies. General Wistar used to say that 'the best form of government is absolutism tempered by assassination'; I think a better form is strong leadership tempered by democracy. Government must have authority, but it should be responsible to the people.

All people are not equally fitted for free-

dom or democracy. It requires not only intelligence and emotional balance, but long
training in the art of living together, to
qualify for the exercise of individual and
social freedom. Children must needs undergo such mental growth and social training
before they can safely be trusted with freedom, and the same is true of societies and
nations. Many so-called democracies are
not really such, but are autocracies or
oligarchies where the people as a whole have
and deserve little freedom in the direction of
affairs. China and Turkey, as well as many
Central and South American countries, were
declared republics before their people were
prepared to exercise the duties of free
citizens. Undoubtedly the same was true in
the early history of this country and in the
extension of the franchise to former slaves.
It was clearly recognized by the founders of
this government that it could rest only on
the intelligence and social training of its

citizens, and hence our system of public education. Even general intelligence is not enough, for it requires long training in the ways of democracy to learn to abide by majority rule and to trust to the slow processes of education and persuasion rather than to compulsion in correcting evils of government. No doubt a wise and beneficent dictatorship could correct social evils and hasten social progress more rapidly than the slow processes of democracy. But the history of dictators, past and present, leaves one doubtful of their wisdom or beneficence and more than doubtful as to the permanent value of their governments. For after all there is a larger purpose in government than to secure quickly some desired good. Whether it be in the case of children or of nations, the ultimate purpose of government should be education for freedom. It is in this sense that 'a free government is better than a good government,' as Lincoln said.

3. *Co-operation by Compulsion or Persuasion*

The greatest problem of organized society is how to achieve co-operation. The oldest as well as the newest solution of this problem is by means of force. This method of forced co-operation was used in all of the extinct civilizations of the past. It was the method of the builders of the Pyramids, of Oriental potentates and Roman Cæsars, and it is the method of present dictators. It can succeed for a time even now by abolishing representative government, suppressing freedom of speech and press and even of thought and conscience, cultivating war-psychology and intense nationalism, and by prostituting science, education, and religion for purposes of propaganda. But there is little reason to suppose that it can succeed in the long run, especially in an era of general enlightenment and among people who have once breathed the air of freedom.

The other method of securing social co-
operation is by means of democracy rather
than autocracy, persuasion rather than
compulsion, reason rather than emotion,
education rather than propaganda. This
method is slow and inefficient in a crisis and
at such times free men often submit to the
authority of commanders and dictators only
to return to freedom and democracy in
normal times. Freedom from slavery of
body, mind, and spirit has been bought at
too great a price through long ages of conflict and martyrdom to permit sane men to
discard it permanently at the order of a
dictator or a mob. One of the amazing revelations of this post-war period is the com-
pliant way in which millions of people in
different countries of Europe have surren-
dered all freedom, not only in government,
but also in speech, press, thought, and
conscience; but surely this cannot be for
long. Surely this war-psychosis will run its

course and frenzied emotion give place to reason.

At its meeting in Boston in December 1933, the American Association for the Advancement of Science adopted the following 'Declaration of Intellectual Freedom' which should, I think, occupy an honored place alongside of our Declaration of Independence:

> The American Association for the Advancement of Science feels grave concern over persistent and threatening inroads upon intellectual freedom which have been made in recent times in many parts of the world.
> Our existing liberties have been won through ages of struggle and at enormous cost. If these are lost or seriously impaired there can be no hope of continued progress in science, of justice in government, of international or domestic peace; or even of lasting material well-being.
> We regard the suppression of independent thought and of its free expression as a

major crime against civilization itself. Yet oppression of this sort has been inflicted upon investigators, scholars, teachers and professional men in many ways, whether by governmental action, administrative coercion, or extra-legal violence. We feel it our duty to denounce all such actions as intolerable forms of tyranny.

There can be no compromise on this issue, for even the commonwealth of learning cannot endure 'half slave and half free.'

By our life and training as scientists and by our heritage as Americans we must stand for freedom.

Of course balance must be preserved here as everywhere in life. Freedom must be balanced by responsibility; the one is directly proportional to the other and each reacts upon the other so that the greater the freedom the greater must be the responsibility and *vice versa*. But unless biology, history, and philosophy are false guides, there is no permanent place in the modern world for such exhibitions of tyr-

anny as some nations of Europe are making.
These are surely blind alleys from which
they must in time return to the paths of
progress.

III

WHAT'S WRONG WITH THE WORLD?

1. *'Man's Inhumanity to Man Makes
Countless Thousands Mourn'*

Every day the newspapers make us
aware that many things are wrong, and
seriously wrong, with our human world.
In international relations we read of wars
and rumors of wars. Desperate fighting in
South America, slaughter of defenseless
men, women, and children; vast prepara-
tions for war in Japan, Russia, Germany,
Italy, France, England, and even America.
Violations of treaties and peace pacts; failure
of disarmament conferences; higher tariff
walls; increasing national isolation and
international antagonisms; crushing taxa-

tion to pay for past, present, and future wars; and back of all this, international suspicion, fear, and hate.

In national affairs we learn of class, sectional, and racial conflicts; labor arrayed against capital, agriculture against industry, colored races against white, or white against colored; Moslems against Hindus, Nazis against Jews.

In forms of governmental organization we hear of social revolutions, of autocracy at war with democracy, communism fighting fascism, socialism arrayed against capitalism, dictatorships overthrowing representative governments; denials of all individual freedom, not only in government, but also in press, speech, thought, and even in religion; imprisonment, and even death for those who are unwilling to become slaves of a bureaucracy.

In personal and public relations our papers are filled with accounts of murders and kidnapings; dishonesty and graft in high places, public officials whose motto is, 'public office is a private snap'; criminal bankers, politicians, lawyers; racketeering, hijacking, blackmailing; strikes, picketing, and lockouts; 'malefactors of great wealth,' and armies of the unemployed begging for food and sleeping in parks under newspaper blankets; luxurious wasters, and starving men, women, and children; widespread poverty and want in a land of superabundant plenty; a civilization unsurpassed in the history of the world for schools, colleges, universities, scientific, cultural, and charitable institutions, and on the other side regiments of human wrecks, bums, and thugs crowded into jails, penitentiaries, reformatories, asylums, hospitals and almshouses.

No doubt this is a one-sided account; millions of peaceful, law-abiding, unselfish, and altruistic communities and individuals do not make 'news,' while scores or hundreds of the other sort do. But, even so, something, no, many things must be seriously wrong with the world. No one facing these facts can truthfully say, 'God's in his heaven, all's right with the world.' It is no wonder that sensitive people sometimes try to shut these evils out of their eyes and minds and prefer to turn to more pleasant thoughts, to dwell upon the good that is in the world rather than the evil. It is no wonder that scholars and scientists often try to shut out all this discord and bury themselves in their studies. Even in the golden age of Greece, Euripides wrote:

'Blessed is he who has gained knowledge of nature,
Who seeks neither the woes of citizenship
Nor rushes into unjust deeds,
But who observes the ageless order of immortal nature,
Asks how it was constituted and when and why!
To such the practice of base deeds never cleaves.'

It is not surprising that in the face of all these evils many religions have turned to

the contemplation and consolations of a
future life of peace, happiness, and right-
eousness; while many who would reform
society condemn religion and science for
permitting such conditions to exist. Recently Henry A. Wallace, the present
Secretary of Agriculture, has criticized scientific men for their failure to notice or take
part in correcting the evils of unemployment
and of undistributed goods and wealth
which they have so largely created, while
many religious leaders and organizations
are condemning the churches for their
smug conservatism and are calling their
members to live and work for 'peace on
earth, good will to men.'

Wrongs cannot be righted by ignoring
them, and here, as in every other matter,
the only hope of improvement is in finding
the causes of these human disharmonies
and in removing or restricting those causes.
This is the method of science in dealing

with all classes of phenomena. Physics, chemistry, and biology are ever seeking the causes of phenomena, and when these are found it is often possible to bring these phenomena under control. Modern medicine in particular is now able to control or mitigate many diseases by finding their causes and removing or modifying them. And if social diseases and disorders are ever to be remedied, it must be done in this same way.

What then are the causes of these social disorders? Undoubtedly there are a legion of them, big and little causes, near and remote ones; they are often attributed to the war, the depression, prohibition, *et omnes genus*. But while these may have intensified present disorders, they do not explain the ever-present lack of harmony among men. What are the underlying causes of human hate and greed, of the inhumanity of man to man, of class, racial, and national antagonisms?

2. *The Struggle for Existence and the Natural Inequalities of Men*

The first and most widely accepted answer has ever been, 'Because the world, man's world in particular, is made that way.' It is the law of the jungle, the survival of the fittest, the natural inequalities of men. Good and evil exist in the nature of things. Men are wise or fools, honest or dishonest, rich or poor, because of Fate — Ἀναγκη of the Greek, Kismet of the Moslem, Foreordination of the Calvinist, Heredity of the scientist. Undoubtedly there is some truth in this answer, although it is not the whole truth. There is in nature a widespread struggle for existence. Nature has endowed some men more richly than others. Heredity reaches back through countless generations of ancestors, and the hereditary constitution of every individual is fixed at the time of the fertilization of the egg from which he developed. Some persons are blessed with a good inheritance, while others are cursed with inherited tendencies to epilepsy, feeble-mindedness, insanity, or criminality. Some are blessed with good environmental influences before and after birth, others are blasted by dwarfing and degrading conditions over which they have no control.

The natural differences of heredity and environment among individuals and nations and races, coupled with the ever-present struggle for existence, are said by fatalists to be the irremediable causes of the evils and disharmonies in the world of men. We know that in the world of plants and animals heredity and environment produce dwarfed and defective individuals, beasts of prey and their victims, parasites and their unwilling hosts, fighting and destructive animals, warring colonies of ants and raiding packs of wolves. Nowhere is there universal good, for what is good for one is often evil for another and there is little altruism in nature that extends beyond the species concerned. All of these things seem to confirm the opinion that disharmony and evil exist in the nature of things.

No doubt the nature of things is responsible for much of the evil that exists in the world of nature and of men, but it is also true that man is learning to control conditions and causes so as to prevent evils, to improve on nature, and to turn to his own benefit the destructive and hostile forces of nature. Ever since man first domesticated the savage wolf and converted it into man's best animal friend, or first cultivated the wild grasses and converted them into wheat and other cereals, he has been engaged in improving on nature. What are all the advances in medicine and surgery, in nutrition and sanitation, in education and social organization, but improvements on primitive nature? Indeed, civilization and all of its institutions are man's products, the work of his hands and mind. And as all of the useful and progressive inventions and customs of society are man-made, so also many of the evil and destructive ones are man-made, and can therefore be unmade by man. Of course human society is founded upon inherited reactions and instincts, for which man is not directly responsible, but upon this natural foundation human intellect and purpose have built many good and also many evil customs and institutions.

Heredity is not the inexorable fate it is often pictured, for it furnishes only the foundation of personality, and upon this foundation environmental conditions, including education and human purpose, build the developed character of every person. Heredity determines only capacities and possibilities, environment determines which of those possibilities will become realities. In the heredity of every person are many alternative possibilities, some good, some bad; which of these will be realized as actualities depends upon environment, education, human purpose. In short, the claim that wars can never cease because man is by nature a fighting animal neglects the fact that man can to a certain extent control nature and rise above fate.

3. *The Devil in Man vs. Natural Causation*

A second answer to the question, 'What's wrong with the world?' is found by some persons in the Devil, 'original sin,' or an evil will or spirit outside or inside man. This also is one of the primitive beliefs of mankind, found among most savages and even among many enlightened persons. Probably this view is based upon the fact that the causes of which we are most conscious are those which we attribute to our own wills. In our experience good seems to be the result of good will, evil, of evil will, and accordingly we are apt to ascribe all evil to big or little devils, outside or inside man.

In the earlier stages of human culture all disease and suffering were thus ascribed to evil or malignant powers, and medicine-men undertook to propitiate the evil spirits by human or animal sacrifices, or to exorcise them by magic, incantations, or torture. Formerly insane persons were thought to be possessed of devils, and to drive out the devils they were bound with chains, burned with fire, scourged with lashes, or sprinkled with holy water; more recently they have been immured in padded cells, put into straitjackets, had their hands chained or fastened in leather muffs, gagged when they screamed, or beaten when they were unruly or disobedient. With increasing knowledge of the natural causes of diseases, whether of the body or the mind, these

savage methods of treatment have been replaced by modern medicine, which by
scientific and rational methods seeks to
remove these causes.

Contrast the methods of science in con-
trolling natural phenomena by dealing with
their causes with the methods of governments in dealing with international discord;
or the methods of medicine in treating bodily ills with those of politics in dealing with
social ills; or the methods of modern education in training the lame and blind and
feeble-minded with those of many so-called
reformatories and penitentiaries (note the
good intentions of these words) in dealing
with social offenders. Governments do not
usually seek to find the causes of international or racial hostilities and then strive
to remove those causes. On the contrary,
their acts are frequently provocative rather
than conciliatory. There is often great international friendship shown and expressed

in after-dinner speeches, and a callous disregard for the rights and feelings of neighbors in acts of governments. In some great catastrophe that overwhelms a people, as in the great earthquake and fire in San Francisco, or in Tokyo, the heart of the world is stirred to sympathy and assistance, but in seeking commercial, territorial, or nationalistic advantage the law of the jungle prevails.

The United States is, as we know, a peace-loving nation, sincerely desirous of cultivating friendly relations with other nations, and yet in our business dealings with them we have little use for the golden rule, but much for the iron rule of doing to others as they do unto us, or even for the brass rule of 'doing our neighbor and doing him well,' rather than good. Sometimes we are the Santa Claus among the nations and sometimes Uncle Shylock. At times we are really good Samaritans, and again we pass by on the other side with the Pharisees. For example, we deeply and needlessly offended the Japanese by our abrupt cancellation of the 'gentlemen's agreement' concerning immigration and the adoption of the Japanese Exclusion Act, in which we denied to that nation the quota system prescribed for all other nations except China. Prince Tokagawa told me in 1926 that Japan had no criticism to offer of our policy of restricting immigration, indeed he thought that the United States should have restricted immigration twenty-five years earlier, but there was serious criticism of the fact that Japan was not treated as other nations were. He said the quota system applied to Japan would have permitted the admission of less than two hundred immigrants per annum, whereas probably more than that number came in illegally after the cancellation of the 'gentlemen's agreement.' We have thus deeply offended a nation that once regarded us as their best friend without any advantage whatever to ourselves. In similar manner and on various occasions our government has needlessly provoked other nations when it might have achieved better and more lasting results by conciliatory methods. It is true that most of these unfriendly acts are the results of bad judgment rather than of hostile intent and that they are frequently forced on the nation at large by insistent minorities rather than by the will of a majority of the people, but when we pride ourselves on being the most peaceful and friendly nation on earth, it is well for us to try to see ourselves as others see us. The fact is that almost all nations sincerely desire peace, but they are unwilling to pay the price of peace which is merely the universal price of friendship among neighbors, namely, the avoidance of unnecessary offense and the determination to find and remove, as far as possible, the causes of fear, suspicion, and hate.

Precisely the same principles apply to race, class, political and religious conflicts within a nation. They can be controlled only by finding their causes and eliminating them as far as is possible. Of course differences of opinion will always exist among freemen, for unfortunately as intelligence increases differences of opinion increase. The basal human emotions are much the same in all classes and conditions of men. All living things are forever seeking satisfaction; all human beings are ever seeking animal, intellectual, social satisfactions. The highest and most enduring satisfactions of human life are freedom to seek truth, beauty, service, and thus to find a more abundant and enduring life. But while the emotions of mankind are everywhere much the same, rational processes differ greatly, owing in part to the fact that they are so largely the products of environment and education, whereas basal emotions are more largely the products of heredity. In short, emotional unity is greater than rational unity. This fundamental fact is taken advantage of by all governments in times of crisis. In war, political contests, and social revolutions appeals are made to emotions rather than to reason. Differences of opinion are not dealt with objectively but subjectively. Opponents of Nazis or Fascists or Communists often maintain that their reasoning is not only false in fact, but that it springs from evil intentions, and similar charges are hurled by each of these groups against all others. Conflicts of labor and capital are generally ascribed to evil will and purpose, rather than to objective causes. Crime is held to be the result of devilish wills, evil natures, bad heredity, and it is commonly supposed that the only way to improve these is to destroy them altogether. Therefore, it is held that force, force to the uttermost, must be used to promote harmony.

4. *Emotional vs. Rational Conceptions of Punishment*

The old conception that evil is the result of evil intent naturally led to the practice of retributive justice and vengeful punishment. The evildoer was treated so as to drive out or destroy his evil spirit, rather than to correct, or if possible convert, his evil will into peaceful and useful purpose. Prisons, chains, torture, thumbscrews, racks, gallows, guillotines, electric chairs were used to throw terror, or what is sometimes euphemistically called 'the fear of God,' into religious and political heretics as well as into criminals. To a certain extent the old *lex talionis*, an eye for an eye, a tooth for a tooth, a life for a life, still prevails in the attempt to 'make the punishment fit the crime.' This conception of retributive justice has cursed society from its beginning. It is entrenched in law, government, and even religion.

More civilized conceptions of punishment seek to make the punishment fit the criminal rather than the crime. The only rational use of punishment is for the correction of the offender or the protection of society. When punishment hardens the offender and turns him out a worse enemy of society than when he was punished, it is accomplishing no good. If the protection of society demands it, there is no sufficient reason why dangerous characters should be turned loose on society. The correction of the offender should always be the first aim of all justice, but the improvement and protection of society should always be its final aim. The relative failure of some of the most modern systems of reformation of young criminals is clearly shown in a recent study by Dr. and Mrs. Gluck of five hundred criminal cases in the Concord, Massachusetts, Reformatory, and in a later study of one thousand juvenile delinquents. Some eighty-eight per cent of these youthful offenders continue their lives of crime after their release. The Reformatory, in short, fails in most cases to reform. Either the offenders are incorrigible or something is wrong with the system. Probably both of these alternatives are true in certain cases. Maudlin sentimentalism concerning the inalienable rights of life, liberty, and the pursuit of happiness for criminals as well as normal citizens often turns loose on society human beasts of prey merely because they have served their time. Protection of society, not punishment of the offender, should be the chief aim in all cases where it is impossible to re-educate and reform the criminal.

No doubt bad heredity, leading to weak or evil wills, is one of the causes of crime. But bad education and example, bad social customs and habits have more to do with making bad men than bad heredity. It is fortunate that this is so, for these conditions can be more readily controlled than can heredity. It would take many generations, perhaps thousands of years, markedly to improve human heredity, even if the breeding of men could be strictly supervised. There is no known method of improving heredity except the method used by animal and plant breeders of selecting the best stock for breeding and eliminating not only the worst but even the poorer stock from reproduction; and apart from the difficulty, if not the impossibility, of applying these methods of breeding to the human stock, mankind is at present such a mongrel race, good and bad heredity are so widely spread in the general population, and the rate of reproduction is so slow that it would certainly take thousands of years to make any marked improvement in the human stock by these methods. But time is long, man is inventive, and the future may see great improvements in human heredity.

But although it is almost impossible at

present to eliminate bad heredity, at least one vastly important thing can be done, namely, to see that social conditions and customs are so improved that the best stocks do not become extinct. This is one of the greatest dangers that threatens high civilization at present, namely, the elimination of its most promising lines, and this can be prevented if only the more intelligent and progressive men and women can be made to realize that the most important service that they can render to society is to leave worthy descendants in the world. When once our social customs or fashions are so changed that it will be considered immoral for people with serious hereditary defects to have children, and when on the other hand it will be said of apparently superior persons who have no children that they must have some hidden physical, mental, or social defects, since they are childless — when this time comes, if it ever comes, we shall have the most practical system of eugenics that can be applied to the human race.

But in its present serious situation the world cannot wait for the slow improvement of human heredity, while it is possible at once so to improve environment as to get much more out of our inherited capacities than is now done. Environment and education can be vastly improved. One of the greatest tragedies of life is the fact that many persons with inherited potentialities of genius and leadership are so dwarfed in their development by hard conditions of poverty, lack of education, closed doors of opportunity, that their inherited capacities never have a chance to come to full fruition. Occasionally we see a great genius like Beethoven, Faraday, or Lincoln rising superior to these adverse circumstances and becoming a world figure. But for every such fortunate individual there must be many others of great potential value who remain undeveloped and unknown. These are the 'mute, inglorious Miltons' of the world, those 'whose hands the rod of empire might have swayed,' if only their inherent powers could have found a chance to develop.

5. *The Major Social Importance of Environment and Education*

My work as a biologist has been largely in the field of embryology and it has led to the study of development under many different conditions. It is surprising what changes can be produced in one and the same organism by changes in its environment during its development. For example, the great differences in structures and habits of the workers and queens of ants and bees, or of the various castes of workers and soldiers in a colony of termites, are caused not by heredity but by the kind and amount of food supplied to the larvæ, and there is no doubt that early environmental influences have a profound effect upon human development. Usually the earlier these conditions act the more profound are their effects. This simply confirms the age-old maxim, 'As the twig is bent the tree inclines.' Education is the attempt to influence development through the control of environmental factors.

As a result of many years of experience as a teacher, I have come to believe that the most important effect of education is habit-formation. Indeed, I am not sure that there is any other permanent result of education except the formation of good habits and the suppression of bad ones. Heredity is our first nature, habits are second nature, and once established they become a permanent part of our characters. Good or bad habits of body, mind, and morals shape very largely the whole personality. There are bodily habits of health or invalidism, skill or bungling, industry or sloth; mental habits of accuracy or guessing, zeal or indifference, responsibility or irresponsibility, success or failure; moral habits of sincerity or pretense, cheer or gloom, helpfulness or selfishness, temperance or debauchery. It is the aim of good education to develop the first of each of these and to suppress the second. This can be done only by each person for himself; all that friends, parents, or teachers can do is to supply suitable stimuli, the subject must make the response. And as the proper response is made again and again, the habit becomes formed and fixed so as to be really second nature. Education is thus an active and not a passive process. No one can be given an education. Information can be given but not development, inspiration but not character, stimuli but not response. Habits make or mar the whole life. There are sometimes students in school or college who think it smart to beat the system designed to develop good habits; instead they cultivate

habits of inattention, loafing, cheating, irresponsibility, apparently unconscious of the
fact that they are injuring chiefly themselves.

6. *Reciprocal Relations of Freedom and Responsibility*

Responsibility is ability to respond to
stimuli in certain prescribed or desirable
ways and it is always based upon ability to
choose between alternatives. Where there is
no such ability there can be no responsibility. Responsibility varies with intelligence;
that is, the capacity to profit by experience.
Feeble-minded or insane persons or young
children are not equally responsible with
normal, intelligent adults, while an increasing burden of responsibility rests upon those
of superior intelligence. This burden is
rarely if ever a comfortable one. We desire
ease, it drives us to work; we want pleasure
and it frequently causes pain; and therefore
many persons go through life shirking re-

sponsibility and 'passing the buck.' Such behavior leads to paralysis of effort and failure in life. Too often we fail because we do not try. On the other hand, responsibility assumed and discharged leads to ever greater and greater responsibility and success. It is the most important factor in building character.

Freedom and responsibility characterize societies no less than individuals and in general the ills of society can be mitigated or cured by aroused public opinion. Nations no less than individuals may develop habits of helpfulness or selfishness, friendliness or hostility, peace or war. Most of our social evils are the result of bad social habits that could be changed if there were sufficient desire to change them.

As one of the results of a false idea of development there is current among some scientists and philosophers the view that man is a mere automaton, the helpless creature of heredity and environment over which he has no control, and that one is born to success or failure, service or uselessness, virtue or vice; that one has no control over his development, but is merely a pawn in the hands of Fate, and has therefore no responsibility for his character or destiny. This paralyzing philosophy is false both in theory and fact. In the evolution of higher animals and in the development of every normal human being there has been a birth and growth of freedom. When memory and intelligence become factors in behavior, they introduce a new dispensation of freedom from rigid, instinctive responses. Such freedom is proportional to intelligence, while heredity, instincts, and habits limit freedom. No person is responsible for his heredity or early environment; these are fixed beyond his power to change or alter. But when he arrives at an age when he can make conscious, intelligent responses to stimuli, he can by *taking thought* suppress certain responses and favor others and thus become a free moral agent. We are neither absolutely free nor absolutely bound. Heredity and early environment have set bounds about us that we cannot pass, but within those bounds we do have a certain degree of freedom and responsibility.

Multitudes of people have little self-control and some scientists and philosophers deny that there is any such thing. But their own lives belie such a paralyzing philosophy. They may spend laborious days and years in accomplishing some plan or purpose, they may work until it hurts, holding on to the limit of their strength, and yet in their philosophy maintain that they could not have done otherwise; but in actual life and experience they would resent any claim that they were irresponsible and therefore deserved no credit for their accomplishments. The fact is that such a philosophy of irresponsibility cannot be lived. Actual experience proves that we are not mere automata. Chance, heredity, early environment over which we have no control have done much to shape our lives and characters, but education, training, and habits may be consciously cultivated so as greatly to modify the entire personality — body, mind, and will. Man is thus able to rise above fate and say with Ulysses:

> 'That which we are we are,
> One equal temper of heroic hearts,
> Made weak by time and fate, but strong in will
> To strive, to seek, to find and not to yield.'

IV

The Present Crisis in Civilization

In the long history of living things on the earth there have been innumerable crises in the lives of individuals and species as well as in human societies and civilizations. Many of these crises have ended in degeneration or extinction, others have led to progress.

The word 'crisis' means a turning-point, the parting of ways, the opening or closing of doors of opportunity. Living things are forever meeting crises; they are always choosing, either consciously or un-consciously, between alternative paths in their search for satisfaction. Organized human societies are now facing one of the major crises in the history of mankind which may mean either failure and degeneration or further and greater progress.

In an address on this War Memorial Foundation I cannot fail to deal with our responsibility in meeting this crisis in civil-ization, and especially our responsibility to those who gave their lives as they hoped to end war and to make the world safe for de-mocracy. Cynics may scoff at these phrases, but can any serious person scorn these ideas? Differences of opinion as to the best method of attaining these goals must be expected, but surely no differences exist as to their desirability or necessity, if our civilization is to be preserved. The seal of this War Memorial Foundation shows one who has fallen passing to another who is pressing on, not a sword or gun, but the torch of enlightenment, and it bears the motto, 'The Cause shall not Fail.' — What cause? Not victory in war, nor national aggrandizement, nor selfish isolation, but rather the cause of peace and human progress.

We are facing today one of the greatest crises in the history of civilization, but we stand so near these current events and are so much a part of them that it is difficult for us to realize their portentous importance. The World War was probably the greatest man-made catastrophe in the entire history of the human race. During this dreadful conflict sane men everywhere said, 'This must never happen again. This is a war to end war.' But now only sixteen years after its close it seems that it has only ended

peace.   The spirit of national co-operation
among allies has ended in national suspicion
and isolation; social integration has under-
gone disintegration; the fires of mutual
service and sacrifice have gone out and left
the ashes of selfishness, greed, and hate.

For a time the United States held a unique
position of leadership among the nations of
the earth and it looked as if our nation might
be the chief factor in restoring the world to a
rational peace, but the hate and fear en-
gendered by the war were too strong for the
peace-makers. President Wilson's 'fourteen
points,' which would have helped to re-
store peace, were ridiculed here and abroad
and were scrapped at Versailles. He fondly
hoped that the League of Nations would
serve to bring the nations together and to
prevent future wars, but partisan rancor
and his own unwillingness to compromise
led our Senate to refuse to enter the League
of Nations and instead to cling to an anti-

quated and impossible policy of isolation. In a world where time and space have virtually been annihilated and where all nations are necessarily neighbors, some of our leaders thought that they could build up walls around America so that we could prosper whatever might happen to the rest of the world. For us no League of Nations, no World Court, no foreign entanglements! But the entanglements exist and cannot be avoided. And now for five years millions of our citizens have been learning through bitter experience that we cannot prosper while the rest of the world suffers. Now that the League of Nations has been greatly weakened by our refusal to co-operate and by the withdrawal of Japan and Germany, even our isolationists are wondering what can take the place of the League in preventing war. Certainly it has been demonstrated that disarmament conferences, treaties of arbitration, and peace pacts without means

of enforcement will not do it. Our influence
and power in preserving peace, joined with
that of the other nations, and especially with
the English-speaking ones, might well have
prevented war and the threat of war in the
Orient and Europe. Apparently if the leading nations of the world will not combine
against war, they must prepare for the next
war. The whole world is now so bound together by science and invention, by trade
and finance, even by fear of war and the
crushing financial burdens that it entails,
that nations must co-operate or perish.

America cannot safely avoid its great
responsibility in helping to maintain the
peace of the world, and the time to preserve
peace is before it is broken. We know from
bitter experience that in any general and
prolonged war our country cannot remain
isolated and preserve its neutrality. National isolation is no longer possible for us;
we must either co-operate in maintaining
peace or prepare for war.

This dreadful situation, with the world drifting toward war, has stimulated certain student bodies in England and America to poll college and university students with respect to these three questions: (1) Would you refuse to take part in any future war? (2) Would you take part only to repel invasion? (3) Would you answer any call of your country to arms?   Approximately twenty-three thousand replies from sixty-five colleges in the United States showed that more than one third of this number would refuse to take part in any war; one third would fight only in defense of American soil; while less than one third would answer any call of their country to arms.[1] Anti-war societies have been established in many colleges and the students in the largest and most progressive institutions are leaders in this movement. Antagonism to military

[1] A much more complete canvass of student sentiment on these questions is now being made by the Association of College Editors and the *Literary Digest*.

courses is widespread and parades and demonstrations for peace are marked by such enthusiasms as usually characterize athletic victories. Similar demonstrations against war and for peace are occurring in the English universities and neither in these nor in American institutions is it any longer a stigma of dishonor to be known as a pacificist. Undoubtedly this movement on the part of large numbers of educated young men and women who will be leaders in the English-speaking world when the next war threatens is a powerful factor for peace, and a promise that 'the Cause shall not fail.' Unfortunately in many countries the youth movement and student organizations are strongly militaristic. In Italy, Germany, Russia, Finland, and Japan they form the most aggressive and warlike part of the population, and in Cuba and some Latin-American countries they are leaders in armed revolution.

The strong stand against war taken by leading clergymen and churches in America is having a great effect on public opinion, and the vigorous action of the General Federation of Women's Clubs protesting against the unlimited sale of arms and the building-up of great armaments is another sign that the threat of war is here meeting with widespread resistance. Most of all, the amazing revelations that have been published recently showing that the munition manufacturers and armament makers of Germany, England, France, Italy, Czechoslovakia, and America are the never-ceasing causes of war, that they continually stimulate national antagonisms, defeat disarmament conferences, sell their products impartially to friend and foe, are the enemies of all nations and yet are protected by all, and that their only patriotism is for dividends and bonuses — these revelations are opening the eyes of thousands to one of the most potent causes of war. The recent action of President Roosevelt in calling for an embargo on the shipment of military supplies to Bolivia and Paraguay ought to be followed by all nations and should be extended to the armament business in general. It is intolerable that a relatively small number of munition makers should be permitted to continue to disturb the peace of the world and to drag bleeding nations at their chariot wheels, all for private gain. If this nefarious business could be stopped, it would probably do more than any other single thing at this time to prevent war.

But the permanent elimination of this great threat against civilization must be sought in education. War and social disorders in general are not so much the results of bad heredity as of bad education; they are therefore much more easily controlled. Formal education has of late given too little attention to the intelligent training of the emotions and the will. The result is that man has learned to control the vast forces of nature better than his own spirit. Education must hereafter concern itself more with the cultivation of good social habits and the elimination of bad ones. Indeed, education is the chief hope of human progress, but it must be liberal and ethical rather than selfish propaganda.   Unlike the announced new German system, it must glorify peace rather than war, sympathy rather than hate, humanity rather than nationalism. Instead of teaching personal and national selfishness and greed, it must teach tolerance, sympathy, generosity; instead of teaching narrow, parochial patriotisms, it must teach the universal brotherhood of man.

Good social habits can be learned as well as good mental and bodily habits. Education that leads to the development of ethical character is more important in this world crisis than is the mere increase and diffusion of knowledge. The world cannot wait for the slow improvement of human nature through eugenics, although that also must come in the distant future. But, as I have said before, heredity determines only capacities and potentialities, while the development of those potentialities depends upon environment and training. The capacities of good social development are already present in all normal persons, but they must be developed by good environment and education.

We often hear it said that you cannot change human nature, that man is by nature a fighting animal, and that, therefore, wars will never cease. It is true that we cannot change inherited human nature except by the process of eugenics, but we can change human nurture, or development, and this has been done again and again. The chief difference between civilized men and savages is due to their environment and education rather than to heredity. Cannibalism, human sacrifices, polygamy, the burning of heretics, the torture of witnesses, the duel, and a thousand other social customs of former times have been banished from civilized society by better education, not by improved nature or heredity; and war can also be banished by the same means. H. G. Wells has said that the fate of civilization depends upon the race between education and degeneration; civilization will survive only if education wins.

Fortunately the opportunities for world-wide education were never so good as they are today. The printing press, the telegraph, the telephone, radio, moving pictures, rapid transit on land and sea and in the air have put information concerning the whole world within the reach of everyone in free countries. World opinion can now be formed and expressed, not years and centuries after an event, but while it is happening, and although nations may at times be so under the control of emotion that they refuse to listen to reason, no nation can long stand against the sober judgment of the majority of mankind. Japan and Germany are even now showing that they are sensitive to world opinion, and in the end they cannot fail to be influenced by it. Today more than ever before there is great force in what our Declaration of Independence so finely expresses in the phrase, 'A decent respect to the opinions of mankind.'

But these vast opportunities for education may be used for false propaganda, as well as for truth, for promoting war as well as peace, and in the present dictatorships of Europe where every means of information is carefully controlled, it is difficult or impossible for people to learn the truth except perhaps as the result of long and bitter experience. Lincoln's shrewd saying that 'You can fool all of the people some of the time and some of the people all of the time, but you cannot fool all of the people all of the time,' would not be true where all means of information and education are in the hands of dictators. In such cases nothing but the failure of dictatorship and the suffering of the people will bring enlightenment. But there is good historical evidence for the belief that in the long run 'truth is mighty and will prevail' in spite of dictators, censors, and propagandists. Enlightenment, either by rational processes of education or by the slow and severe methods of trial and error, is the only road of permanent social progress.

This is no easy nor rapid cure for the ills of the world, but it is the only rational one. Science and education, knowledge and ethical character are the chief hopes of human progress. To be effective for lasting good, knowledge must rest upon ethical character. Unless the instincts and habits of service, sympathy, and love overcome selfishness, greed, and hate; unless the ideals of altruism, justice, and brotherhood are cultivated and prevail; unless freedom, responsibility, and democracy survive, neither navies nor armies nor world power can save our civilization.

'Far called our navies melt away,
    On dune and headland sinks the fire,
And all our pomp of yesterday
    Is one with Nineveh and Tyre.
Lord God of Hosts, be with us yet,
Lest we forget, lest we forget.'